Baking Bread

AUDREY ELLISON

A QUINTET BOOK

ISBN: 0–7858–0489–7

This book was designed and produced by
Quintet Publishing Limited

Art Director: Peter Bridgewater
Designer: Melanie Williams
Editors: Fanny Campbell, Josephine Bacon
Baking by Jacksons of Saxmundham, Suffolk
Photographers: Trevor Wood, Michael Bull
Jacket Design: Nik Morley

Typeset in Great Britain by
Central Southern Typesetters, Eastbourne

Produced in Australia by Griffin Colour

Published by Chartwell Books
A Division of Book Sales, Inc.
P.O. Box 7100
Edison, New Jersey 08818–7100

CONTENTS

Introduction

All types of bread supply a significant portion of carbohydrate, protein and B vitamins to the diet. Wholewheat and brown breads provide more dietary fibre than white bread. Bread also supplies calcium, phosphorus and iron. Flour with an extraction rate of 80% or less of the bran and wheatgerm is fortified with the B vitamins thiamine (B1) and nicotinic acid and iron to compensate for milling losses. Brown and white flours also contain added calcium. As the recipes in this book indicate, the varieties of bread are numerous and display a wide spectrum of textures and flavours, plain and enriched, sweet and savoury. The home baker is able to cater for special requirements such as salt-free bread, gluten-free bread, milk- and wheat-free breads and breads, buns and fruit loaves free of artificial colouring and flavouring as indicated in hyperkinetic diets. There is a growing consumer preference today for wholewheat breads. Some 25% of the bread consumed in English-speaking countries is now non-white.

• BREAD-MAKING INGREDIENTS •

The flour most commonly used in bread-making is wheat, but rye, barley, oats and triticale (a hybrid of wheat and rye) are alternatives. Bread may be made from a single flour or a mixture of two or more flours. Wheat is prized for its fine baking qualities. There are three main types of wheaten flour: *wholewheat* containing the whole of the wheat grain with nothing added or taken away, an extraction rate of 100%; *brown* containing about 85% of the wheat grain (a similar flour is known in the USA as graham flour); and *white* containing about 75% of the wheat grain. Most of the bran (i.e. the outer fibrous layers of the grain) and the wheat germ are removed in the milling process. The term stoneground, sometimes applied to flours, means that the flour is ground between two stones instead of being milled by the modern steel-roller-mill process.

Gluten is composed of insoluble proteins which absorb water and produce a fine network of elastic strands. Carbon dioxide is produced by yeast fermentation and this raises the bread. The gluten stretches to give the loaf its bold volume. Flour used in yeast cookery should be plain and not the chemically aerated self-raising (self-rising) type. In Europe the so-called strong flour gives the best breadmaking results because of its higher gluten content. The texture of loaves made from wholewheat and brown flours is closer than that of white bread. The volume is also usually less in the wholewheat and brown bread types because of the effect of the higher bran content on gluten elasticity.

Strong flour has a gluten content of up to 12½%. It should be used for bread-making in the UK. Elsewhere, plain or all-purpose flour is the best for bread-making. However, if the raising (rising) agent for the bread is baking powder, any kind of flour — even self-raising (self-rising) — can be used. Throughout this book, the recipes do not specify a gluten content for the flour. Use the most suitable bread flour that you can find.

Liquids used in dough-making The liquid in a dough usually consists of water or milk (which may be skimmed or whole, dried or fresh). Some baking-powder breads utilize sour milk and buttermilk which react with the raising agent for a lighter dough. Less commonly, wort (a yeasty liquid made from hops), beer and even blood provide the liquid ingredient as in some Scandinavian breads, for instance. Liquids for yeast doughs are usually added when lukewarm.

Eggs are added to doughs to enrich them nutritionally. They also improve the keeping properties and colour of the baked product.

Raising agents. Fresh baker's yeast consists of unicellular organisms which, under suitable conditions of temperature, moisture and food supply, break down the sugar in dough, forming carbon dioxide and alcohol. Fresh yeast is moist, grey-cream in colour and free from a dry, brown covering of dead cells. Yeast works best at blood heat (body temperature). Blend the fresh yeast with dough liquid at 38°C/100°F. It is unnecessary to add sugar when blending fresh baker's yeast with liquid. Cold temperatures slow down yeast activity as do doughs containing a lot of fat, sugar and salt. Slow rising is often desirable, as it improves the flavour and texture of the bread; it may be achieved by placing the dough in a refrigerator for several hours at a time. Suitably wrapped fresh baker's yeast (in amounts most frequently used) may be stored in the refrigerator for about three weeks or in a freezer for up to six weeks. If too much yeast is used in a dough, it produces a sour, yeasty flavour and a smell of alcohol. The bread becomes stale quickly and is crumbly in texture.

Dried yeast (dry or active dry yeast) is convenient to store — up to four months in an airtight container. Check the date stamp when purchasing it. Dried yeast has a shelf life of 4 to 6 months. Reconstitute dried yeast with some of the warm dough liquid (at 38°C/100°F) and a small quantity of 'starter' sugar or follow manufacturer's instructions if they are different. Leave in a warm place until the yeast dissolves and the mixture becomes frothy. Certain new brands of dried yeast are mixed directly with the flour. The package instructions will also tell you how much dried yeast will raise what amount of flour. Follow manufacturer's instructions if these conflict with the recipe.

The sponge batter technique This method is applied to enrich yeast doughs where the amounts of fat, eggs and sugar slow down the fermentation process. The use of a sponge batter helps to overcome the slowness.

Prepare the sponge batter by adding the yeast (and a little sugar in the case of dried yeast) to warm liquid. Stir in a small amount of the flour to make a batter. If dried yeast is used, allow some 5 to 10 minutes for the yeast to foam before flour is added.

Set the batter aside in a warm place for about 20 minutes to enable the yeast to ferment. The fat, eggs and sugar are then added to the foaming batter and mixed to a soft dough.

Leaven (sourdough) is a fermentation agent seldom used in home-baking today. It is made from dough which has been allowed to lie and ferment naturally, thereby producing yeast cells and lactic acid bacteria. The final product flavour results from normal yeast activity combined with the sour lactic acid taste. Nowadays, even in the San Francisco area, sourdough starter is usually made under laboratory conditions, to prevent impurities entering the bread.

Chemical substances used to lighten doughs include bicarbonate of soda (baking soda) which needs to combine with an acidic ingredient such as sour milk or buttermilk, as in Irish soda bread.

● BAKING EQUIPMENT ●

The equipment for baking consists of a large glass, earthenware or stainless steel bowl, a wooden fork and mixing spoon, a rubber or plastic spatula, a rolling pin, polythene (plastic) sheets, 2 pastry brushes, oven cloths or gloves, cake rack and baking (cookie) sheets, loaf tins (pans), a measuring jug (cup) and a set of measuring spoons, a sieve for icing (confectioner's) sugar, weighing scales and a grater for citrus rinds.

Loaf tins (pans) and flowerpots are useful for shaped loaves. They should be prepared before use to prevent sticking. Grease tins (pans) and baking (cookie) sheets with unsalted cooking fat (shortening) or dust thoroughly with flour. The greased tins (pans) may also be dusted with cracked wheat, semolina or bran flakes. Non-stick tins (pans) are ready for use without greasing.

Earthenware (not plastic) flowerpots need to be washed thoroughly and dried. Coat them with cooking fat (shortening), inside and out, and then bake in a hot oven for 5–10 minutes. Allow to cool and repeat the process 3 or 4 times. The pots are then ready for use. Grease prior to half-filling with dough. Wipe with damp kitchen paper (paper towel) after use. Electric food mixers with a dough hook accessory are available on the market to facilitate dough-kneading.

● STORAGE ●

Flour is best stored in its bag on a cool, dry, airy shelf. If larder or store cupboard conditions are damp, put the flour bag into a plastic box with a well-fitting lid or pour the flour into a clean, dry, covered jar. Avoid mixing new flour with old.

Plain white flour keeps up to one year. Self-raising (self-rising) flour, and wholewheat and brown flours keep for 2 to 3 months.

When a drum of yeast is half-used, it is better to transfer the residue to a smaller container (such as a small, dark-glass jar) rather than have a large air space over the yeast. Chemical aerating agents require cool, dry storage. The practice of transfer to smaller, well-sealed containers also applies to baking powder.

Breads vary in their keeping properties. Crusty loaves are best eaten freshly baked. Enriched breads, milk, malt and rye breads keep fresh for several days. The storage life depends on the recipe formula and the storage conditions.

Unwrapped bread is best stored at room temperature in a clean, airy, dry container such as a bread crock or bin. The container should not be airtight. Bins and crocks should be cleaned and dried weekly, or crusts and crumbs may promote mould (mold) growth. Unsliced bread may be put into a clean, dry, plastic bag for storage. Wrapped bread should be left in its wrapper. Leave the wrapper loosely folded so that air can circulate.

Bread can stale rapidly if refrigerated, since moisture may be lost. Freezer storage of suitably wrapped bread is very successful in most cases. Plain breads (brown and white) may be kept in a freezer for about 6 months, enriched loaves for 4 months. Crusty loaves (French or Vienna) may shed their crusts after a few days. Frozen bread may be thawed in a microwave oven and sliced bread may be toasted directly from the freezer.

Stale bread loaves and rolls may be refreshed by wrapping in foil and heating for 5 to 10 minutes in a preheated oven at 230°C/450°F/Mark 8. Allow the bread to cool in the foil. Crusty varieties should not be covered but placed in a hot oven for 5 to 10 minutes. Serve it warm. Stale bread is better than fresh bread for use in cooking, and it is easier to grind into breadcrumbs.

• BAKING TECHNIQUES AND METHODS •

Prepare baking tins (pans) and trays in advance.

Fermented doughs Cream the yeast, fresh or dried, with the warm dough liquid. Add the yeast liquid to the flour and *mix* by hand or with a wooden dough fork.

Knead the dough with the heel of the right hand on a lightly floured board, folding the dough in half towards you, then pushing it down and away from you. Using the fingertips of the left hand, give the dough a quarter turn and repeat the folding and pushing movements with the heel of the right hand. The soft, sticky dough gradually becomes smooth and elastic and loses its stickiness. White doughs require about 10 minutes kneading, wholewheat and brown doughs only about 4 minutes (even less for quick brown doughs).

Kneading may also be done using a food mixer or processor according to the manufacturer's instructions.

If the dough is very soft, beat it with a wooden spatula, or in a food mixer, until smooth and elastic.

The kneaded dough is allowed to rise until doubled in size. Normally the dough is allowed to rise twice, first after kneading and then after shaping. Quick methods of bread-making cut out this first rising stage and reduce the overall time to

1¾ hours. The method involves the use of vitamin C in the dough, 25 mg vitamin C is added to 600 g/1½ lb white flour. It is added to the dough liquid. Dough which is left to rise must be covered. The traditional floured tea-towel or cloth is replaced nowadays with oiled polythene. The dough may be placed in a large, oiled, polythene bag or plastic bin-liner (trash bag) or the dough bowl may be covered with a sheet of oiled polythene. In this way the surface of the dough remains soft and no crust forms over it. The speed at which the dough rises depends upon the surrounding temperature, the slower the better from the flavour point of view. Suitable places include a warm place such as a kitchen or airing (hot) cupboard (or even a car parked in the sun!) to the cool of the refrigerator. Dough may need only one hour to rise in a warm place (up to 32°C/90°F), 1½–2 hours at room temperature (18–21°C/65–70°F), 3½–4 hours in cool conditions and up to 12 hours in a refrigerator. Reduce by half the quantity of yeast used if rising takes place in the refrigerator or the dough will be difficult to handle and the product will taste yeasty when served. However warm the environment, if the atmosphere is too damp or the weather thundery, this can affect the rising.

Before the final stages of dough-handling, ensure that the oven is preheated to the correct temperature. Plain doughs require an oven temperature of 230°C/450°F/Gas 8 and enriched doughs 200°C/400°F/Gas 6.

The second kneading process is known as *knocking back*. The aim is to obtain a product with good, even texture. The knocking back ensures that large air bubbles are broken up and the air redistributed. Nutrients for the yeast cells are also redistributed and made more readily available. Knead the dough as before and then shape into loaves or rolls, as required.

The shaped items (on baking trays, in baking tins (pans) or flowerpots) are lightly covered with oiled heavy polythene (plastic) sheeting and set aside to prove for ½–1 hour (according to the volume of the items to be baked). The dough becomes light and doubles in size.

Bake in a very hot oven in order to kill the yeast cells. The loaves, rolls or buns should rise well, look brown and crisp and feel light. Loaves tapped on the base should sound hollow. Bread may be tested by inserting a skewer into it. If the skewer is dry when withdrawn, the bread is baked. Loaves may be removed from their tins (pans) some 5 minutes before the end of baking if crisp results are needed.

• READY MIXES •

Products for preparing yeasted wheaten doughs (including pizza-base mixes) and soda breads, using both white and brown flours, are obtainable. When purchasing wheaten dough powder, check the label to see if it includes yeast. If not, this must be bought separately. Follow the instructions on the packet (package).

Prepared doughs of various kinds are obtainable deep-frozen, ready to put into the oven. They may even be ready meals, deep-frozen or chilled, such as pizzas, with a yeast dough base. Thawing may be carried out in a microwave oven, but baking results are usually best using an ordinary domestic oven.

Basic Yeast Bread Doughs

• QUICK WHITE BREAD •

INGREDIENTS
2 tbsp/50 g/2 oz fresh yeast or 4 tbsp/25 g/1 oz dried yeast and ½ tsp sugar
3¾ cups/750 ml/1½ pints warm water
2 25 mg tablets (pills) vitamin C
12 cups/1.5 kg/3 lb white flour
2 tsp salt
2 tbsp sugar
¼ cup/50 g/2 oz butter or margarine
Oven temperature 230°C/450°F/Gas 8
MAKES 2 LARGE (OR 4 SMALL) LOAVES

● Grease two large (or four small) bread tins (pans). Mix the yeast with a few tablespoons of the water adding the teaspoon of sugar if dried yeast is used. Set the dried yeast liquid aside for 10 minutes until frothy. Crush the vitamin C tablets (pills) in a little water and add to the yeast liquid.
● Mix the flour and salt together in a large warm bowl. Add the sugar and rub in the fat. Stir in the yeast liquid and the rest of the warm water and mix to a soft dough. Turn on to a lightly floured board and knead the dough until it is smooth, elastic and

non-sticky. Divide the dough in half, shape into 2 or 4 loaves and put them into the bread tins (pans). Cover the tins (pans) with oiled polythene (plastic) and prove until doubled in size, about 1 hour. Remove the polythene (plastic) and bake the loaves for about 45 minutes (30–35 minutes for small loaves). Cool the bread on a wire rack.

• WHITE BREAD •

INGREDIENTS
1 tbsp/25 g/1 oz fresh yeast or 2 tbsp/15 g/½ oz dried yeast and 1 tsp sugar
3¾ cups/900 ml/1½ pints warm water
12 cups/1.5 kg/3 lb white flour
2–3 tsp salt
1 tbsp sugar
¼ cup/50 g/2 oz butter or margarine
Oven temperature 230°C/450°F/Gas 8
MAKES 3 LARGE LOAVES

● Grease three large bread tins (pans). Stir the yeast with a few tablespoons of the water adding the teaspoon of sugar if dried yeast is used. Put the bowl of dried yeast liquid aside for 10 minutes until frothy. Mix the flour and salt together. Add the sugar, rub in the fat, stir in the yeast liquid and the rest of the warm water to make a soft dough. Turn the dough on to a lightly floured board and knead until it becomes smooth, elastic and non-sticky. Return the dough to the bowl, cover it with oiled polythene (plastic) and allow to prove until doubled in size, about 1¼ hours. Knock back the dough and divide it into 3 portions. Knead and shape into loaves to fit into the three bread tins. Cover the bread tins with oiled polythene (plastic). Allow to prove until doubled in size, about 45 minutes. Remove the polythene (plastic) and bake the loaves for 45–50 minutes. Cool on a wire rack.

• WHOLEWHEAT BREAD •

INGREDIENTS

3 tsp/40 g/1½ oz fresh yeast or 3 tbsp/20 g/¾ oz dried yeast and 1 tsp sugar

3¾ cups/900 ml/1½ pints warm water

12 cups/1.5 kg/3 lb wholewheat flour

2–3 tsp salt

1 tbsp sugar

¼ cup/50 g/2 oz butter or margarine or 4 tbsp vegetable oil

beaten egg, milk or salted water for glazing

cracked wheat, bran or buckwheat for decorating (optional)

Oven temperature 230°C/450°F/Gas 8

MAKES 3 LARGE LOAVES

● Grease three large (2 lb/1 kg) bread tins (pans). Stir the yeast into a few tablespoons of warm water, adding the teaspoon of sugar if dried yeast is used. Set the dried yeast liquid aside for 10 minutes until frothy. Put the wholewheat flour into a large mixing bowl and add the salt and sugar. Rub in the fat and stir in the yeast liquid and the rest of the warm water. Mix well and turn on to a floured board. Knead the dough until it is non-sticky. Return the dough to the bowl, cover it with oiled polythene (plastic) and leave it to prove in a warm place for about 1¼ hours, until doubled in size. Knock back the dough. Divide it into 3 portions and shape into loaves to fit into the bread tins. Cover the bread tins with oiled polythene (plastic) and allow them to prove in a warm place for about 40–45 minutes, until doubled in size. Remove the polythene (plastic) and brush the tops of the loaves with the selected glaze. Sprinkle the loaves with grain if desired.

● Bake for 45–50 minutes. Cool on a wire rack.

NOTE: The proving takes some 15–30 minutes longer if carried out at room temperature.

• ALTERNATIVE SHAPES •

Instead of putting the dough into a flowerpot or large (1 kg/2 lb) bread tin (pan) it may be shaped in various ways as loaves or rolls. White bread may be shaped in the same way.

COB LOAF Shape the dough into a large ball. Flatten it slightly and place on a greased baking (cookie) sheet. Slash the top of the dough with a sharp knife to make a cross. Cover and prove for about 45 minutes in a warm place. Bake for 30–40 minutes.

ROLLS (makes 12) Baking time for rolls is 10–15 minutes after shaping, proving and glazing.

PLAIT (BRAID) Divide the dough into three equal pieces. Roll each piece into a strand 30–35 cm/ 12–14 in long. Pinch together one end of the three strands and then plait (braid) them. Pinch the remaining ends together and lift the plait (braid) on to a greased baking (cookie) sheet. Cover, prove and glaze as for the flowerpot loaf. Decorate with poppy seeds, if desired. Bake for 25–30 minutes.

COTTAGE ROLLS Cut off one-third of each 50 g/2 oz piece of dough. Shape each piece into a ball. Place the large ball on a baking sheet and put the smaller one on top. Push a floured wooden spoon handle through both pieces of dough.

DINNER ROLLS Shape each 50 g/2 oz dough piece into a ball or sausage shape. Place on a baking sheet.

CLOVER LEAF ROLLS Divide each 50 g/2 oz piece of dough into 3 equal parts. Shape into 3 balls. Place on the baking sheet in the shape of a clover leaf and press lightly together.

THREE-STRAND PLAITED (BRAIDED) ROLLS Cut off 50 g/2 oz pieces of risen dough. Divide and roll each piece into three 10 cm/4 in strands. Plait (braid) as above.

TWO-STRAND PLAITED (BRAIDED) ROLLS Divide the 50 g/2 oz dough pieces in half. Roll each piece into a strand 20 cm/8 in long. Place the strands in the form of a cross on the work surface. Take the two ends of the lower strand and cross them over the middle of the upper strand so that they lie side by side. Repeat this with the remaining strand and repeat alternately until all the dough has been used. Pinch the ends firmly together. Place on the baking sheet, glaze and decorate, cover, prove and bake.

KNOT ROLLS Roll 50 g/2 oz pieces of dough into a thick 15 cm/6 in strand. Tie into a simple knot.

Currant Loaf

Garlic Bread

INGREDIENTS

2 tbsp/25 g/1 oz fresh yeast or 1 package dried yeast and
1 tsp sugar

1¼ cups/300 ml/½ pint warm skimmed milk
(or warm milk and water)

4 cups/450 g/1 lb flour

2 tbsp sugar

1 tsp salt

2 tbsp/25 g/1 oz butter or margarine

⅔ cup/100 g/4 oz currants

warm honey for glazing

Oven temperature 190°C/375°F/Gas 5

MAKES 2 LOAVES

● Grease two small loaf tins (pans): 20 × 10 × 6 cm/
8 × 4 × 2½ in. Stir the yeast into the warm milk
(add the spoonful of sugar if the yeast is dried).
Leave until frothy, about 10 minutes in the case of
dried yeast. Mix the flour, sugar and salt together
and rub in the butter. Add the currants and pour on
the yeast liquid. Work to a firm dough which no
longer clings to the bowl.
● Turn the dough on to a lightly floured board and
knead until it is smooth and elastic, about 5 minutes.
● Put the dough back into the bowl, cover it with
oiled polythene (plastic) and prove for about 45
minutes or more, until doubled in size.
● Knock back the dough on a lightly floured board.
Divide the dough into 2 halves. Roll out each piece
into an oblong shape, then roll it up (like a Swiss roll
or jelly roll). Place each roll into a loaf tin. Cover
them with oiled polythene, then leave to prove for
1–1¼ hours until doubled in size. Bake the uncovered loaves for 40–45 minutes.
● Turn the loaves out on to a wire rack and brush
the tops of the bread with warmed honey. Cool and
serve with butter.

NOTE: Milk Bread dough may be used as the
basis for the currant loaf instead of the
dough recipe above. Simply add the currants to
one-third the quantity of dough.

INGREDIENTS

1 French stick or Vienna loaf

⅓ cup/75 g/3 oz butter

1 to 2 cloves garlic, crushed with a little salt or put
through a garlic press

Oven temperature 200°C/400°F/Gas 6

● Slice the bread slantwise and thickly, but do not
cut through the bottom layer of the loaf. Cream the
butter together with the crushed garlic. Spread both
sides of each slice with the garlic butter and also
spread garlic butter over the crust of the loaf. Wrap
the loaf in foil and heat the parcel in the oven for
10–15 minutes.
● Serve Garlic Bread hot with soup or salads.

Flowerpot Loaf

INGREDIENTS

2 tsp/15 g/½ oz fresh yeast or 1 package dried yeast and 1 tsp sugar

2 cups/200 g/8 oz strong white flour

2 cups/200 g/8 oz wholewheat flour

1 tsp sugar

1 tsp salt

1 tbsp/15 g/½ oz lard

1¼ cups/300 ml/½ pint warm water

Oven temperature 230°C/450°F/Gas 8

(Brown bread, using a quick wholewheat dough)

● Grease two 4–5 in/10–13 cm flowerpots which have been seasoned . If they are not available, grease a loaf tin (pan), 9 × 7½ × 2½ in/ 23 × 13 × 6 cm, instead.

● Blend the fresh yeast in the warm water or dissolve the dried yeast in the warm water to which a teaspoonful of sugar has been added. Set aside for about 10 minutes until frothy.

● Put the flours, sugar and salt into a large, warmed mixing bowl and rub in the lard. Add the yeast liquid and mix to a soft dough.

● Turn the dough onto a lightly floured board and knead until smooth and non-sticky.

● Divide the dough in half and put a piece into each pot. Place the pots on a baking sheet. Cover the pots with oiled polythene and leave to rise in a warm place until the dough has doubled in size (50–60 minutes). Remove the polythene. Brush the loaves with milk or salted water and sprinkle with cracked wheat.

● Bake for 30–40 minutes until done and loaf responds with a hollow sound when the bottom of the bread is tapped.

● Cool the loaves on a wire rack.

● Flowerpot loaves owe their delicious flavour to the tasty crust which develops over the whole surface of the bread.

Blender Oatcakes

INGREDIENTS
3 cups/250 g/8 oz rolled oats (fine oatmeal)
2 cups/450 ml/¾ pint hot water
10 dates, stoned (pitted)
1 tbsp/25 g/1 oz fresh yeast or 1 package dried yeast and 1 tsp sugar
2 cups/250 g/8 oz wholewheat flour
½ tsp sea salt
Oven temperature 200°C/400°F/Gas 6
MAKES ABOUT 30 OATCAKES

● Grease 2 baking (cookie) sheets. Grind the rolled oats (oatmeal) to a flour in an electric blender. Then remove it from the blender. Put the water and dates into the blender and blend until smooth. And the yeast or yeast and sugar to the warm mixture and set aside for 5 minutes.

● Stir the oat flour into the yeast mixture. Add half the wholewheat flour and the salt. Beat vigorously, then stir in the rest of the wholewheat flour.

● Drop tablespoons on to the baking (cookie) sheets and let rise for 20–30 minutes in a warm place until doubled in size.

● Bake for 15 minutes. Lift from the baking sheets with a spatula and stack on wire racks to cool.

Pita

Pita bread is of Middle Eastern origin and readily available in many food stores nowadays. Pita may be made from white flour or from wholewheat. It may be split in half for filling while hot and packed with small pieces of meat, such as kebabs, and salads. It may also be served as an accompaniment to dips such as hummus and taramasalata. Serve pita hot.

INGREDIENTS

1 tbsp/15 g/½ oz fresh yeast or 1 package dried yeast and ½ tsp sugar
1¼ cups/300 ml/½ pint warm water
4 cups/450 g/1 lb white flour
1 tsp salt
Oven temperature 240°C/475°F/Gas 9
MAKES 8 PITA BREADS

● Grease two baking (cookie) sheets. Stir the yeast into the warm water, adding the sugar if dried yeast is used. Leave dried yeast for about 10 minutes in a warm place to become frothy.

● Stir the salt into the flour and mix to a dough with the yeast liquid. Knead thoroughly on a lightly floured board for about 10 minutes until the dough is smooth, elastic and non-sticky. Return the dough to the warm bowl and cover with oiled polythene (plastic). Prove in a warm place until doubled in size, about 1¼ hours.

● Knock back the dough. When thoroughly kneaded, divide the dough into 8 pieces. Roll each portion into an oval shape 25 × 13 cm/10 × 5 in. Put the 8 pitas on baking sheets. Cover with oiled polythene (plastic) and set aside to rest for 5–8 minutes. Bake for 6–8 minutes. (Do not overbrown as, if not eaten freshly baked, the pitas are reheated before serving.) Wrap the pitas in a clean, damp tea (dish) towel to cool to make them soft and pliable.

Scotch Baps

Crumpets

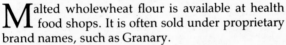

Malted wholewheat flour is available at health food shops. It is often sold under proprietary brand names, such as Granary.

INGREDIENTS
2 tsp/15 g/½ oz fresh yeast or 1 tbsp/10 g/¼ oz dried yeast and 1 tsp honey
1¼ cups/300 ml/½ pint skimmed milk or water
4 cups/450 g/1 lb malted wholewheat flour
1 tsp salt
2 tbsp vegetable oil
sifted flour for dusting the baps
Oven temperature 200°C/400°F/Gas 6
MAKES 6 BAPS

INGREDIENTS
2 tsp/15 g/½ oz fresh yeast or 1 package dried yeast and ½ tsp sugar
1¼ cups/300 ml/½ pint warm water
3 cups/350 g/12 oz white flour
1 tsp salt
½ tsp bicarbonate of soda
⁷⁄₈ cup/200 ml/7 fl oz warm milk (more, if required, to make a pouring batter)
MAKES ABOUT 20 CRUMPETS

● Grease and flour a baking (cookie) sheet. Mix the yeast with a few tablespoonfuls of the warm milk, adding the teaspoonful of honey if dried yeast is used. Set the dried yeast liquid aside for 10 minutes until frothy.

● Put the malted wholewheat flour into a warm bowl, add the salt and stir in the oil. Mix to a soft dough with the yeast liquid and the remaining milk.

● Knead well on a lightly floured board until the dough becomes springy and non-sticky. Return to the bowl, cover with oiled polythene (plastic) and prove in a warm place, about 35–40 minutes, until doubled in size. Knock back the dough.

● Divide the dough into 6 pieces and roll them out on a lightly floured surface into oval shapes about 1 cm/½ in thick. Place on the baking sheet. Dredge the tops with flour. Cover with a sheet of oiled polythene and leave to rise until doubled in size, about 40 minutes. Bake for 20–25 minutes. Cool on a wire rack. Dust again generously with sifted flour before storing.

● Heat a greased griddle or heavy frying pan (skillet). When ready to cook the batter, grease crumpet rings, egg-poaching rings or plain biscuit (cookie) cutters 7.5 cm/3 in in diameter. Stir the yeast into the water, adding the sugar if dried yeast is used.

● Let the dried yeast liquid stand for 5–10 minutes until frothy. Mix in half the flour and beat well. Set the batter aside in a warm place for about 30 minutes until foamy.

● Add the rest of the ingredients to the batter, stirring thoroughly. Beat well, adjusting the milk quantity if necessary.

● Place the crumpet rings on the heated griddle and pour 2 tablespoonfuls of the batter into each ring. Cook until set underneath and holes appear on the upper surface. Take away the rings and turn the crumpets with a palette knife (spatula). Lightly cook the second side. Cool the crumpets stacked on a wire rack. Serve freshly made with butter or toast them on both sides, serving them hot with butter, later on.

Crown Loaf

Oven temperature 230°C/450°F/Gas 8

● Grease an 18-cm/7-in (or 15-cm/6-in) sandwich tin (shallow cake pan). Break off six ¼ cup/50 g/2 oz pieces of two, three or more of the preceeding doughs. Work each piece into a ball, using the palm of the hand. Place five balls to form a circle in the sandwich tin (shallow cake pan) and the sixth in the centre. Cover, prove and bake in the usual way.

NOTE: Three cups mixed doughs make 2 Crown Loaves.

• MARBLED BREAD •

An effective loaf may be baked from a mixture of bread doughs such as 1 cup/225 g/8 oz each of the following: Quick Wholewheat dough, plain risen White dough, risen White dough to which 3 tablespoons chopped herbs (dill and parsley) have been added, risen white dough containing 2 tablespoons tomato purée (paste), and quick Wholewheat dough containing half a ripe banana, mashed, plus 1 tablespoon honey. Countless other variations are possible, both sweet and savoury. Toppings such as cracked wheat, bran, rye flakes, barley flakes, poppy seeds, sesame seeds etc, may also be varied and more than one type used on the same loaf.

Muesli Bread

INGREDIENTS
1 tbsp/25 g/1 oz fresh yeast or 1 package dried yeast and 1 tsp sugar or honey
3¾ cups/750 ml/1½ pints warm water
6 cups/675 g/1½ lb white flour
4 cups/450 g/1 lb wholewheat flour
2 tsp salt
¼ cup/50 g/2 oz margarine
2 cups/225 g/½ lb unsweetened muesli
cracked wheat or bran for decoration

Oven temperature 220°C/425°F/Gas 7

MAKES 3 LARGE LOAVES

● Grease three large flowerpots or three large bread tins (pans) and sprinkle them with cracked wheat or bran.
● Stir the yeast into the water, adding the sugar or honey if dried yeast is used. Set aside for about 10 minutes to become frothy. Mix the white and wholewheat flours together with the salt (and sugar, if used). Rub in the margarine. Pour in the yeast liquid and mix thoroughly. Turn the dough on to a floured board and knead until smooth and elastic. Cover the dough in the bowl using a sheet of oiled polythene (plastic) and allow to prove in a warm place until doubled in size (1–1¼ hours). Turn the dough on to the floured board and knock it back after working in the muesli.
● Divide the dough into 3 portions and shape them to fit the flowerpots or bread tins (pans). Brush the dough with milk and cover with oiled polythene (plastic). Prove for about 40–50 minutes until doubled in size.
● Bake for 45–50 minutes. Cool on wire racks.

Herb Bread

INGREDIENTS

2 cups/225 g/8 oz wholewheat flour
2 cups/225 g/8 oz plain (all-purpose) flour
2 tsp/10 g/¼ oz margarine
1 tsp salt
1 tsp sugar
½ tsp dried dillweed
1 tsp dill seed
1 tsp dried savory
2 tsp/15 g/½ oz fresh yeast or 1 package dried yeast and ½ tsp sugar
1¼ cups/300 ml/10 fl oz warm water
cracked wheat for decoration
Oven temperature 230°C/450°F/Gas 8
MAKES 2 LOAVES

● Grease two 18 cm/7 in loaf tins (pans). Mix the flours and rub the fat into them. Add the salt, sugar and dried herbs. Cream the fresh yeast with the water and add to the flour mixture. If dried yeast is used, stir ½ teaspoon sugar into half the dough liquid, sprinkle the yeast on top and leave for 10 minutes in a warm place until frothy. Add with the rest of the water to the flour mixture. Mix to a soft dough and knead on a lightly floured board until smooth. Sprinkle the greased tins (pans) evenly with cracked wheat. Half-fill each tin with bread dough.

● Cover the tins (pans) with lightly oiled cling film (plastic wrap) or polythene (plastic) bags. Allow the dough to rise in a warm place until doubled in size. Uncover the dough and bake in the heated oven for about 35 minutes.

● Remove the loaves from the tins (pans) and serve warm.

Milk Bread

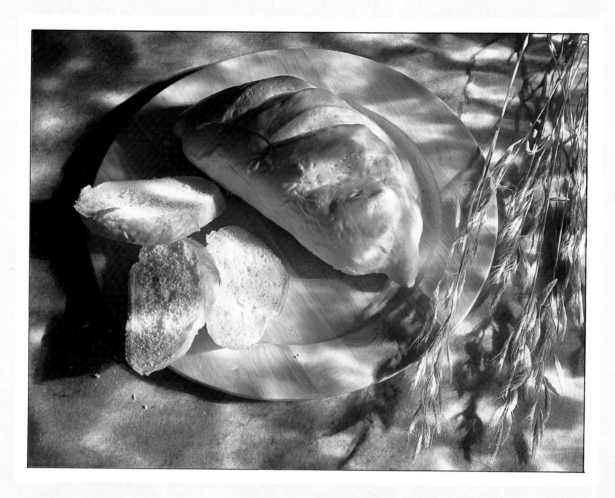

INGREDIENTS

2 tsp/15 g/½ oz fresh yeast or 1 package dried yeast and ½ tsp sugar

2 cups/450 ml/¾ pint warm skimmed milk or whole milk and water mixed

6 cups/675 g/1½ lb white flour

1½ tsp salt

1½ tsp sugar

6 tbsp/75 g/3 oz butter or margarine

beaten egg or milk for glazing

Oven temperature 200°C/400°F/Gas 6

MAKES 3 SMALL LOAVES OR 1 LARGE AND 1 SMALL LOAF

● Grease three small bread tins (pans) (or 1 large and 1 small). Stir the yeast into the liquid, adding sugar if dried yeast is used. Allow 15 minutes in a warm place for dried yeast to become frothy.

● Mix the flour, salt and sugar and rub in the butter or margarine. Stir in the yeast liquid and mix to a soft dough. Turn the dough on to a lightly floured board and knead until it becomes smooth and loses its stickiness. Return the dough to the warm mixing bowl and cover it with oiled polythene (plastic). Leave to rise until doubled in size, about 1½ hours.

● Knock back the dough, divide it into three (or 1 large and 1 small piece) and shape to fit the bread tins (pans). Brush the loaves with beaten egg or milk. Cover the tins (pans) with oiled polythene (plastic) and allow to rise until doubled in size, about 1 hour.

● Bake for about 50 minutes and cool on a wire rack.

VARIATION: OLIVE BREAD Omit the 1½ tsp sugar and stir in 5–6 tbsp olive oil instead of rubbing in the butter or margarine. Add 1½ cups/225 g/½ lb pitted, sliced black olives to the dough with the dough liquid. The olive loaves may be shaped into 2 or 3 rounds and baked on greased baking sheets instead of being baked in bread tins (pans) if preferred.

Naan

This Indian bread is served with tandoori (oven-baked) dishes. As with pita, naan is a yeast-risen flatbread which puffs up on cooking under a very hot grill (broiler), because this creates an air pocket inside the bread.

INGREDIENTS
1 tbsp/15 g/½ oz fresh yeast or 1 package dried yeast and ½ tsp sugar
⅞ cup/200 ml/7 fl oz warm milk
4 cups/450 g/1 lb white flour
½ tsp salt
1½ tsp sugar
1 tsp baking powder
2 tbsp vegetable oil
4 tbsp plain yoghurt
MAKES 6 NAAN

● Stir the yeast into the warm milk, adding sugar if the yeast is dried. Leave dried yeast mixture about 10 minutes in a warm place to become frothy.
● Mix the remaining dry ingredients in a large bowl. Stir in the oil, yoghurt and yeast liquid. Work into a dough. Turn out on to a lightly floured board and knead for about 10 minutes until the dough is smooth, elastic and non-sticky. Return the dough to the warm bowl, cover with oiled polythene (plastic) and leave to prove for about 1 hour in a warm place, until doubled in size. Knock back the dough and, when thoroughly kneaded, divide the dough into 6 pieces. Roll into oval shapes 25 × 10 cm/10 × 4 in and place them on the baking (cookie) sheets.
● Preheat the grill (broiler) a few minutes before baking the naan. Grease two baking (cookie) sheets.
● Cook each naan bread under the hot grill (broiler), 2–3 minutes on each side, until brown and well puffed.

Wheatgerm Bread

To toast the sunflower seeds and wheatgerm, cracked wheat or bran, put them in a dry frying pan (skillet) and heat, stirring frequently, until they start to give off an aroma.

INGREDIENTS

1 tbsp/15 g/½ oz fresh yeast or 1 package dried yeast and 1 tsp honey

1¼ cups/300 ml/½ pint warm water

4 cups/450 g/1 lb wholewheat flour (or ½ quantities of white and wholewheat flours mixed)

1 tsp salt

1 tbsp sunflower oil

½ cup/50 g/1½ oz toasted, chopped sunflower seeds

toasted wheatgerm, cracked wheat or bran for dusting bread tins (pans)

Oven temperature 230°C/450°F/Gas 8

MAKES 1 LARGE OR 2 SMALL LOAVES

● Grease one large or two small bread tins (pans) and sprinkle them inside with toasted wheatgerm.
● Mix the yeast with the warm water, adding the honey if dried yeast is used. Set aside the dried yeast liquid for 10 minutes until frothy. Mix the flour and salt in a large warmed bowl. Stir in the oil, wheatgerm and sunflower seeds. Pour the yeast liquid into the mixture and work into a dough. Turn the dough on to a lightly floured board and knead until the dough is smooth and non-sticky. Shape the dough into 1 large or 2 small loaves and put the dough into the prepared bread tin(s) (pan(s)).
● Cover the tin(s) with oiled polythene (plastic). Leave in a warm place to prove until doubled in size, about 50 minutes. Bake the loaf or loaves for 40–50 minutes, depending on size, until cooked. Cool the bread on a wire rack.

NOTE: The dough may be shaped into 12 rolls and baked for 10–15 minutes on a greased baking (cookie) sheet.

Zürich Weggen

Traditionally eaten by schoolchildren in Zürich on the last day of the summer term, a variety known as Examenweggen.

INGREDIENTS

2 tsp/15 g/½ oz fresh yeast or 1 tbsp/10 g/¼ oz dried yeast and 1 tsp sugar
1¼ cups/300 ml/½ pint warm skimmed milk
¼ cup/50 g/2 oz unsalted butter or margarine, melted and cooled
1 tsp salt
3½–3¾ cups/400–425 g/14–15 oz 81% flour (or white flour)
1 egg, beaten with 1 tbsp milk and 2 tsp sugar for glazing

Oven temperature 220°C/425°F/Gas 7

MAKES 6 LARGE OR 9 SMALL ROLLS

● Grease a baking (cookie) sheet. Crumble the fresh yeast and cream it with 4 tablespoonfuls of the warm milk or sprinkle the dried yeast on the milk containing the teaspoon of sugar. Stir and put the dried yeast liquid aside in a warm place for 10 minutes until frothy. Mix together the melted fat, salt and warm milk. Gradually add the flour and beat thoroughly by hand or for 5 minutes in an elec-

tric mixer. Turn out the dough on to a lightly floured board. Knead for 8–10 minutes until the dough is smooth, soft and elastic. If using a mixer dough hook, knead for 6–9 minutes until the dough forms a ball which is shiny and elastic. Place in a bowl and cover with oiled polythene (plastic). Set aside in a warm place until doubled in size for 45 minutes.

● Knock back the dough. divide into 6 or 9 equal parts. Let the dough pieces rest for 10–15 minutes under oiled polythene (plastic). Shape each piece into a smooth ball. Shape into a long roll, 20–22.5 cm/8–9 in for 6 rolls, 15–17.5 cm/6–7 in for 9 rolls. Roll the lengths to and fro with the palms of the hands. Taper slightly at the ends. Place the rolls on the baking (cookie) sheet, spacing them well. Cover with oiled polythene (plastic) and leave to rise for 35–40 minutes in a warm place until doubled in size. Brush each roll with the glazing mixture.

● Bake the rolls for 10 minutes, then remove them from the oven. Use a sharp knife to make a single slash across the centre of each roll or make a slash lengthwise down both sides, and use scissors to make 5 deep cuts across the top. Push open the cuts.

● Return the rolls to the oven and bake for a further 10–15 minutes, or until brown and shiny. Place the rolls on a wire rack to cool.

Swedish Rye Bread

This slightly sweet-flavoured bread keeps well and makes a delicious accompaniment to cheese.

INGREDIENTS

3 tbsp/75 g/3 oz fresh yeast or 6 tbsp/40 g/1½ oz dried yeast and 1 tsp sugar

2½ cups/600 ml/1 pint warm water

1 tsp salt

1¼ cups/300 g/14 oz treacle

8½ cups/1 kg/2 lb rye flour

2¼ cups/250 g/9 oz white flour

Oven temperature 200°C/400°F/Gas 6

MAKES 1 LONG SWEDISH RYE LOAF

● Grease and flour a deep cake tin (pan) with straight sides, preferably lidded (with a cover) (capacity 6¼–7 US pints/3 litres/5–5½ imperial pints).

● Crumble the yeast into the mixing bowl with a few tablespoons of the water. If dried yeast is used also add the teaspoon of sugar.

● Allow the dried yeast to stand for 10 minutes until frothy. Pour the rest of the warm water over the yeast. Stir in the salt, treacle and rye flour. Add the white flour a little at a time and work the dough until it becomes smooth and non-sticky. The dough should be fairly firm but not stiff. Place the dough into the tin (pan). Cover with a lid or substitute a double layer of foil. Allow the dough to rise in a warm place until about double in size. Bake the bread in a water bath in the oven or over top heat. The water should reach ⅔ of the way up the tin.

● Turn out the loaf and let it cool wrapped in a cloth. Cut the loaf crosswise along the length into 4 portions.

Potato Bread

Barley Bread

INGREDIENTS
1 (225–250 g/8–9 oz) large raw potato
2 cups/450 ml/¾ pint milk
2 tbsp/30 g/1 oz fresh yeast or 1 package dried yeast and 1 tsp sugar
8 cups/1 kg/2 lb flour
2 tsp salt
1 egg
3 tbsp sour cream
Oven temperature 180°C/350°F/Gas 4
MAKES 3 LOAVES

INGREDIENTS
1 tbsp/25 g/1 oz fresh yeast or 2 tbsp/15 g/½ oz dried yeast and 1 tsp brown sugar
2 cups/450 ml/¾ pint warm water
4½ cups/500 g/1 lb 2 oz barley flour
¼ cup/25 g/1 oz soya flour
2 tsp brown sugar
1 tsp salt
1 tbsp vegetable oil
Oven temperature 180°C/350°F/Gas 4
MAKES 2 ROUND LOAVES

● Grease three 6½ × 3½ × 3 in/16 × 9 × 7.5 cm bread tins (pans). Grate the peeled potato finely. Bring the milk to the boil and pour it over the potato in a bowl. Cool until lukewarm and add the fresh yeast. If dried yeast is used stir it, with the sugar, into 3 tablespoons warm milk or water and leave for 8–10 minutes until frothy. Add the dried yeast mixture to the potato–milk mix. Beat in half the flour until well mixed. Add the salt, egg, sour cream and the rest of the flour. Beat the mixture thoroughly. Cover the bowl with oiled polythene (plastic) and set aside in a warm place for 2–2½ hours. Knead thoroughly and divide between the 3 bread tins. Prove once again, covered, for about 40 minutes. Bake for 45 minutes until cooked.

● Grease a large baking (cookie) sheet. Put the yeast into a bowl with ½ cup/125 ml/4 fl oz warm water (and sugar if the yeast is dried). Put in a warm place for about 10 minutes. Put half the barley flour into a warmed bowl and add to it the rest of the lukewarm water, the sugar, salt and oil. Beat thoroughly. Add the yeast liquid and beat once again. Add the soya flour and sufficient barley flour to make a soft dough. Knead on a floured board until smooth.
● Return to the bowl, cover with oiled polythene (plastic) and leave to prove for 20 minutes. Knead and shape into two rounds. Place them on the baking sheet. Cover with oiled polythene (plastic) and prove until doubled in size.
● Bake for 50–60 minutes. Cool on a wire rack.

Tofu Bread

INGREDIENTS

INGREDIENTS
1 tbsp/25 g/1 oz fresh yeast or 1 package dried yeast and 1½ tsp sugar
½ cup/100 ml/4 fl oz warm water
2½ cups/275 g/10 oz wholewheat flour
1 tsp salt
1 medium egg, beaten
2 tbsp melted butter
½ cup/100 g/4 oz tofu
1 tbsp sesame seeds
2 tbsp ground sunflower seeds
Oven temperature 190°C/375°F/Gas 5
MAKES 1 LOAF

● Grease a 6½ × 3½ × 3 in/16 × 9 × 7.5 cm bread tin (pan). Mix the fresh yeast (or dried yeast and sugar) with the warm water. Allow dried yeast to stand for 10 minutes until frothy. Put the flour and salt into a warmed mixing bowl. Stir in the egg, yeast liquid, melted butter, tofu and seeds. Mix well and knead thoroughly.

● Cover the dough with oiled polythene (plastic) and let it stand in a warm place for about an hour until double in size. Knead the dough for several minutes. Shape into an oval and place the dough in the bread tin (pan). Cover as before and allow to rise for about 25 minutes.

● Bake the loaf for about 40 minutes or until golden brown. Cool the bread on a wire rack. Delicious served with herb butter.

Oaten Bread with Sunflower Seeds

INGREDIENTS

3 cups/225 g/½ lb rolled oats (fine oatmeal)
2 tsp salt
4 cups/1 litre/1¾ pints boiling water
3 tsp/40 g/1½ oz fresh yeast or 1 package dried yeast
3 cups/225 ml/8 fl oz warm water
2 tbsp molasses or black treacle
½ cup/75 g/3 oz pitted dates
5 tbsp water
2 cups/275 g/10 oz raisins
1 cup/150 g/5 oz sunflower seeds
3 tbsp gluten (high gluten) flour
6–7 cups/800 g/1½–1¾ lb wholewheat flour

Oven temperature 200°C/400°F/Gas 6 for the first 10–15 minutes, reduced to 190°C/375°F/Gas 5 for 35–40 minutes

MAKES 4 LOAVES

● Grease four bread tins (pans) 6½ × 3½ × 3 in/ 16 × 9 × 7.5 cm.

● Mix together the rolled oats and salt. Pour the boiling water over them and set aside for 1 hour. Dissolve the yeast in the warm water and molasses. Simmer together the dates with the 5 tablespoons water and mash when softened. Add the mashed dates to the rolled oats and yeast mixtures together with the sunflower seeds.

● Stir together the gluten (high gluten) and wholewheat flours and mix them with the other ingredients. Knead to make a smooth dough. Set aside for about 20 minutes in a bowl covered with oiled polythene (plastic). Shape into four loaves and place each into a bread tin. Allow to rise for about 30 minutes and bake.

Oatmeal Bread

INGREDIENTS

1 tbsp/25 g/1 oz fresh yeast or 1 package dried yeast and 1 tsp brown sugar

2¼ cups/500 ml/18 fl oz warm water

4½ cups/500 g/1 lb 2 oz mixed flour (½ wholewheat, ½ white flour)

¼ cup/25 g/1 oz gluten (high gluten) flour

2 tbsp brown sugar

2 cups/175 g/6 oz rolled oats (fine oatmeal)

4 tbsp wheatgerm

4 tbsp soya flour

2 tbsp vegetable oil

1½ tsp salt

Oven temperature 180°C/350°F/Gas 4

MAKES 2 SMALL LOAVES

● Grease two small bread tins (pans). Put the yeast into a bowl (with the sugar, if dried yeast is used) and stir with ½ cup of the warm water. Set aside for up to 10 minutes until foamy. Add the gluten (high gluten) flour, sugar and half the mixed flours to the rest of the water and beat well for 5 minutes. Add the yeast liquid and beat thoroughly. Stir in the rolled oats and set the mixture aside in a warm place for about 30 minutes to make a sponge batter.

● Add the wheatgerm, soya flour, oil, salt and the rest of the mixed flours to the sponge batter. Turn out on to a floured board and knead well until smooth. Return the dough to the bowl and cover with oiled polythene (plastic). Set aside in a warm place until doubled in size, about 30 minutes.

● Knock back the dough on a floured board and divide into 2 pieces. Shape into loaves and place them in the bread tins (pans). Cover with oiled polythene (plastic) and allow to rise until double in size once again. Bake for about 1 hour. Cool on a wire rack.

Bagels

Jewish rolls, which are served split through the centre, buttered and spread with a filling.

INGREDIENTS

1 tbsp/25 g/1 oz fresh yeast or 2 tbsp/15 g/½ oz dried yeast and ½ tsp brown sugar
2 cups/450 ml/¾ pint warm milk
1 tsp brown sugar
¼ cup/50 ml/2 fl oz vegetable oil
2 tsp salt
5 cups/550 g/1¼ lb wholewheat flour (a little extra flour may be needed)
2 quarts/2 litres/3¼ pints water
2 tbsp/25 g/1 oz brown sugar
egg wash for glazing (1 egg yolk plus 1 tbsp water)
toasted sesame seeds, poppy seeds, or sautéed chopped onions for decoration

Oven temperature 190°C/375°F/Gas 5

MAKES 18 BAGELS

● Grease 2 baking (cookie) sheets. Dissolve the yeast in the water, adding the sugar if dried yeast is used. Allow about 10 minutes for dried yeast to rehydrate and the liquid to become frothy.

● Add the brown sugar, oil and salt to the yeast liquid and work in the flour by degrees, beating at first and then kneading the stiffer dough. When all the flour has been incorporated, knead the dough on a floured board for 10 minutes. Return the dough to the warm bowl, cover with oiled polythene (plastic) and allow to rise for about 1 hour until doubled in size. Knock back the dough, cover and prove until doubled in size once again.

● Knock back the dough and divide it into 18 equal pieces. Roll each piece into a strand, 15 cm/6 in long, 2.5 cm/1 in thick, tapering at each end. Shape into rings, pinching the ends firmly together. Cover the shaped bagels and prove for 10–15 minutes. Bring the water to the boil and add the 2 tablespoons of brown sugar.

● Put 2 or 3 bagels at a time into the boiling water and cook until they rise to the surface (takes 1 or 2 minutes). Lift out the bagels with a perforated spoon. Place them on the greased baking sheets.

● Glaze the bagels with egg wash and sprinkle with seeds or onions.

● Bake until browned, about 20 minutes.

Olive Bread

INGREDIENTS

1¼ cups/300 ml/½ pint hot water

3 tbsp honey

1 tsp salt

1 tbsp/25 g/1 oz fresh yeast or 1 package dried yeast

1½ cups/225 g/½ lb pitted olives

2 tbsp dried paprika flakes

½ cup/65 g/2½ oz cornmeal

5–5¼ cups/500 g/1¼ lb wholewheat flour

Oven temperature 190°C/375°F/Gas 5

MAKES 2 LOAVES

● Grease a large baking (cookie) sheet. Add the hot water to the honey and salt and stir to dissolve. Allow to cool to lukewarm temperature and add the yeast. If dried yeast is used set aside for 10 to 15 minutes until frothy.

● Chop the olives coarsely and stir them into the liquid together with the paprika flakes, cornmeal and three-quarters of the flour. Turn the dough out on to a thickly floured board and knead thoroughly until smooth and non-sticky, adding more flour as required. This takes 10 to 20 minutes.

● Shape the dough into a ball and place in the bowl to rise until doubled in size (about 1½ hours) covered with oiled polythene (plastic). Knock back the dough and knead thoroughly. Shape into two rounds and place them on the greased baking sheet.

● Cover with oiled polythene (plastic) once again and set aside in a warm place to prove for a further 40 to 45 minutes. Bake for 30 to 35 minutes.

Soya Bread with Spice and Nuts

INGREDIENTS
1½ cups/175 g/6 oz wholewheat flour
1 cup/100 g/4 oz soya flour, sifted
1 tbsp baking powder
½ tsp salt
2 tbsp brown sugar
1 tsp ground cinnamon
½ tsp ground nutmeg
1 cup/100 g/4 oz chopped almonds
3 tbsp oil
2 medium-sized eggs, beaten
1 cup/225 ml/8 fl oz milk
1 tsp almond essence (extract)
Oven temperature 180°C/350°F/Gas 4
MAKES 1 LARGE LOAF

● Grease a 9 × 5 × 3 in/22.5 × 12.5 × 7.5 cm bread tin (pan). Mix together the dry ingredients and then stir in the oil.

● Pour the milk on to the beaten eggs and add the almond essence (extract). Stir the liquid into the flour mixture. Scrape the dough into the bread tin (pan) and bake for about 1 hour until cooked.

Rye Sourdough Bread

This bread has to be prepared in advance, but is well worth the effort. The starter can be 'kept going' by reserving a piece of the dough and mixing it with a little water and leaving it for a week to ferment until the next batch of bread is made.

SOURDOUGH STARTER

INGREDIENTS

⁷/₈ cup/100 g/3½–4 oz coarse rye flour
1 tsp ground cumin
1 tsp ground fennel
1 tbsp sugar
about ½ cup/100 ml/4 fl oz tepid milk

BREAD DOUGH

INGREDIENTS

3½ cups/400 g/14 oz extra coarse rye flour
2 cups/225 g/8 oz stoneground wholewheat flour
1½ tsp sea salt
1 tsp caraway or cumin seeds
1 cup/250 ml/8 fl oz warm water
2 tbsp milk
Oven temperature 220°C/425°F/Gas 7

● To make the starter, work all the ingredients together. Cover the dough with oiled polythene (plastic) and stand it in a warm place. Knead the dough lightly each day for 3 days, adding a little tepid water if it appears to be drying out. The starter should be ready to use after the third day, but it may be kept in the refrigerator for up to 7 days, until required.

● On the evening before baking, use a large, warmed mixing bowl to combine the flours, sea salt and half the seeds. Make a well in the centre and add the sourdough starter. Add most of the water and mix it in. Sprinkle flour from the sides of the bowl over the liquid. Cover with oiled polythene (plastic) and leave overnight in a warm place.

● On the following day, thoroughly knead the dough. When it is smooth and elastic, shape it into an oblong loaf. Cover the loaf lightly with oiled polythene (plastic) and leave it to prove for 1–1½ hours on a baking (cookie) sheet, in a warm place.

● Brush the loaf with the milk and sprinkle it with the rest of the seeds. Place an ovenproof bowl of water in the oven, and bake the loaf for 50 minutes.

Croissants

Swiss Pear Bread

INGREDIENTS

1 tbsp/25 g/1 oz fresh yeast or 2 tbsp/15 g/½ oz dried yeast and 1 tsp sugar
1 cup/225 ml/8 fl oz warm water
4 cups/450 g/1 lb white flour
1 tsp salt
2 tbsp/25 g/1 oz butter
1 egg, beaten
¾ cup/175 g/6 oz butter (or a mixture of butter and lard), chilled
egg wash for glazing
Oven temperature 220°C/425°F/Gas 7

MAKES 12 CROISSANTS

● Grease two baking (cookie) sheets. Stir the yeast into the water, adding the teaspoon of sugar if dried yeast is used. Stand the dried yeast liquid in a warm place for about 10 minutes until frothy.

● Stir the salt into the flour and rub in the 2 tablespoons of butter. Add the yeast liquid and the beaten egg and work the dough together. Turn the dough on to a lightly floured board and knead until it is smooth and non-sticky. Roll the dough to an oblong 50 × 20 cm/20 × 8 in, making sure that the edges are straight.

● Divide the chilled fat into 3 portions. Dot the first portion over the top two-thirds of the dough, leaving 1 cm/½ in border all round. Fold the dough into three by lifting up the lower part of the dough first of all and covering it with the top, fat-covered third. Seal the edges by pressing them down with a rolling pin. Give the dough a quarter-turn and repeat the rolling and folding twice more, using the second and third portions of fat. If the dough becomes difficult to handle, cover it with cling film (plastic wrap) and let it rest in the refrigerator for about 20 minutes between the rollings. Cover the dough with oiled polythene (plastic) and leave in the refrigerator for 30 minutes. Repeat the rolling and folding 3 times more but without adding fat. Chill in the refrigerator for at least 20 minutes, but the dough at this stage can even be left overnight before rolling and shaping.

● Roll the dough into an oblong 30 × 45 cm/12 × 18 in. Trim the edges. Cut the dough into 6 squares and each square into two triangles. Brush them with beaten egg. Roll up each triangle loosely, towards the pointed end, finishing with the tip underneath. Curve into a crescent shape.

● Place the croissants, well spaced, on the baking (cookie) sheets and brush with egg wash. Cover with oiled polythene (plastic) and prove for about 30 minutes.

● Bake for 20 minutes until golden brown. Cool on a wire rack.

Pear bread is a Swiss Christmas speciality. It keeps very well and in peasant households in former times a whole winter's supply used to be baked on the same occasion.

INGREDIENTS

5 cups/1 kg/2 lb dried pears
1½ cups/250 g/8 oz sultanas (golden raisins)
⅞ cup/100 g/4 oz hazelnuts, chopped
6 tbsp/50 g/2 oz thick candied lemon peel, diced small
1 cup/225 g/8 oz sugar
7 tbsp rosewater
½ glass Kirsch
1 tbsp powdered cinnamon
1 kg/2 lb white bread dough
Oven temperature 220°C/425°F/Gas 7

MAKES 2 LARGE LOAVES (OR 4 SMALL)

● Grease two baking (cookie) sheets.

● Soak the pears overnight in water to cover, then stew them in the water in which they were soaked. Drain and mash the pears removing any stems or cores. Mix the mashed pears with the sultanas (golden raisins), nuts, lemon peel, sugar, rosewater, Kirsch and cinnamon. Knead half the bread dough with the pear mixture and shape into two oblong loaves. Roll out the other half of the dough on a floured board. Divide it in two and wrap each pear loaf inside a sheet of plain dough. Brush the edges of the dough with milk and seal them. Prick the loaves with a fork. Bake for 50–60 minutes.

Bath Buns

If you cannot get coarse sugar crystals, use coloured coffee sugar.

INGREDIENTS

2 tsp/15 g/½ oz fresh yeast or 1 tbsp/10 g/¼ oz dried yeast and 1 tsp sugar
⅝ cup/150 ml/¼ pint warm milk
2 cups/225 g/8 oz white flour
2 tbsp/25 g/1 oz sugar
½ tsp salt
2 tbsp/25 g/1 oz butter or margarine
½ cup/75 g/3 oz sultanas (golden raisins)
3 tbsp/25 g/1 oz mixed dried citrus peel
1 egg, beaten
egg and milk for glazing
2 tbsp/25 g/1 oz coarse sugar crystals or lump sugar coarsely crushed
Oven temperature 220°C/425°F/Gas 7
MAKES 12 BUNS

● Grease 2 baking (cookie) sheets. Stir the yeast (and sugar if the yeast is dried) into the warm milk. If dried yeast is used, allow to stand for 5–10 minutes until foamy. Stir in a quarter of the flour and leave the batter in a warm place for 20–30 minutes.

● To the rest of the flour add the sugar and salt and rub in the fat.

● Stir in the sultanas (golden raisins) and peel. Stir the flour mixture and the egg into the batter. Beat with a wooden spatula or fork for about 5 minutes until the mixture is smooth.

● Cover the bowl with oiled polythene (plastic) and set it aside in a warm place until the contents have doubled in size, about 50 minutes. Beat the dough for 1 minute. Place tablespoonfuls of the mixture on the baking (cookie) sheets, spaced well apart. Brush the tops of the buns with the egg-and-milk glaze and sprinkle with coarse sugar.

● Cover and allow to prove until the buns have doubled in size, about 35 minutes. Remove the polythene (plastic) and bake for about 15 minutes until golden brown.

Chelsea Buns

INGREDIENTS

2 tsp/15 g/½ oz fresh yeast or 1 tsp dried yeast and ½ tsp sugar
6 tbsp/75 ml/3 fl oz warm milk
2 cups/225 g/8 oz plain (all-purpose) flour
½ tsp salt
2 tbsp/25 g/1 oz margarine
1 egg, beaten
2 tbsp/25 g/1 oz butter, melted
½ cup/75 g/3 oz currants or sultanas (golden raisins)
3 tbsp/25 g/1 oz mixed dried citrus peel
¼ cup/50 g/2 oz soft brown sugar
warm honey
Oven temperature 220°C/425°F/Gas 7
MAKES 9 BUNS

● Grease an 18 cm/7 in square baking tin (pan). Stir the fresh yeast into the warm milk. If dried yeast is used, also add the sugar and set aside for 10 minutes in a warm place until frothy.

● Put one-quarter of the flour into a warmed bowl, stir in the yeast mixture and leave in a warm place for about 20 minutes until the batter is foamy.

● Mix the remaining flour with the salt. Rub in the margarine. Stir this flour mixture and the egg into the yeast batter and mix to a soft dough. Turn on to a lightly floured board and knead until smooth. Place the dough in a bowl, cover with a lightly oiled sheet of cling film (plastic wrap) or a polythene (plastic) bag and leave in a warm place until double in size, about 1½ hours.

● Roll out to an oblong strip 30 × 23 cm/12 × 9 in. Brush the dough with melted butter and sprinkle with the dried fruit, mixed peel and brown sugar. Starting from the longer side, roll up the dough like a Swiss roll (jelly roll). Cut into nine slices and place them close together, cut side down, in the baking tin (pan). Cover and leave for about 40 minutes until the buns have doubled in size and joined together.

● Bake for about 25 minutes, until golden brown. Transfer the buns to a wire rack and brush with warm honey while they are hot. Separate the buns when cool.

Brioche

INGREDIENTS

2 tsp/15 g/½ oz fresh yeast or 1 tbsp/10 g/¼ oz dried yeast
and ½ tsp sugar

3 tbsp warm milk

2¼ cups/250 g/9 oz white flour

1 tsp sugar

½ tsp salt

¼ cup/50 g/2 oz butter

2 eggs, beaten

Oven temperature 230°C/450°F/Gas 8

MAKES 12 SMALL BRIOCHES

● Grease 12 brioche tins 7 cm/3 in in diameter.
● Stir the yeast into the milk, adding the sugar if dried yeast is used. Let the dried yeast stand in a warm place for about 5 minutes.
● Stir in ¼ cup/60 g/2 oz flour and the teaspoon of sugar and leave the batter in a warm place for about 20 minutes.
● Mix together the rest of the flour with the salt and rub in the butter. Beat the eggs into the yeast batter. Stir in the dry flour mixture and mix to a soft dough. Turn on to a lightly floured board and knead until smooth and non-sticky. Return the dough to the warm bowl, cover with oiled polythene (plastic) and leave to rise until doubled in size, 1–1½ hours.
● Knock back the risen dough. Divide the dough into 12 pieces. Cut off a quarter of each piece. Shape the larger part of each piece into a ball and place it into brioche tins. Press the centre of each ball to make a hole into which the small piece of dough is placed like a marble. Brush the tops with beaten egg. Cover the 12 tins with oiled polythene (plastic) and set aside to prove for about 40 minutes. Bake for about 20 minutes and cool on a wire rack.

Carrot Bread

INGREDIENTS

2 tsp/15 g/½ oz fresh yeast or 1 tbsp/10 g/¼ oz dried yeast

2 tsp honey

4 tbsp warm water

4 tbsp molasses or treacle

2 tbsp gluten (high gluten) flour

1½ cups/350 ml/12 fl oz warm water

2 carrots, about 175 g/6 oz

1 cup/225 ml/8 fl oz hot water

2 tsp salt

8–9 cups/about 1 kg/2–2¼ lb wholewheat flour

Oven temperature 200°C/400°F/Gas 6

MAKES 2 LARGE OR 4 SMALL LOAVES

● Grease two large or four small bread tins (pans). Add the yeast and honey to the warm water and set aside for about 10 minutes. Blend the molasses (or treacle), gluten (high gluten) flour and the rest of the warm water with the yeast mixture and beat thoroughly. Leave for about 30 minutes until foamy. Grind the carrots in a good processor with the hot water or grate them finely and stir with the water. Add the carrot purée to the yeast mixture. Add the salt and flour and mix to a stiff dough. Knead on a floured board for 10 minutes. Return to the bowl and cover with a sheet of oiled polythene (plastic). Prove for about 30 minutes until double in size. Knock back the dough, cover and again leave to rise until double in size.
● Shape into 2 large or 4 small loaves and place them into the prepared tins (pans). Cover the tins (pans) and leave them to prove for about 20 minutes, until well risen. Bake for about 45 minutes.
● Cool the loaves on a wire rack.

Bara Brith

This Welsh currant bread has an attractive speckled appearance.

INGREDIENTS

1 tbsp/25 g/1 oz fresh yeast or 15 g/½ oz dried yeast and 1 tsp sugar
1 cup/225 ml/8 fl oz warm milk
4 cups/450 g/1 lb plain white (all-purpose) flour
1 tsp salt
1 tsp mixed spice
6 tbsp/75 g/3 oz butter or margarine
6 tbsp/75 g/3 oz soft brown sugar
1 egg, beaten
3 cups/425 g/15 oz mixed dried fruit (currants, sultanas (golden raisins), raisins, candied citrus peel)
warm milk and honey for glazing

Oven temperature 220°C/425°F/Gas 7, reduced to 180°C/350°F/Gas 4

MAKES 1 LARGE LOAF

● Stir the yeast into the warm milk. If the yeast is dried, add the sugar and set aside for about 10 minutes until foaming. Add ½ cup of the flour and beat well. Set the bowl aside in a warm place for 20 minutes to produce a foamy batter. Mix together the rest of the flour with the salt and spice. Rub in the fat and add the brown sugar. Add the flour mixture and the beaten egg to the yeast batter and knead the dough, first in the bowl and then turned on to a floured board. Knead until the dough is smooth. Return the dough to the bowl. Cover it with a sheet of oiled polythene (plastic) and prove for 1½ hours in a warm place. Work the dried fruit into the dough, knead and shape to fit into the bread tin (pan). Brush the dough with warm milk and honey and cover with oiled polythene (plastic). Prove for a further 1–1¼ hours, until the dough is doubled in size.
● Bake at the higher temperature for 15 minutes. Then bake for a further 45 minutes at the lower temperature. Turn the loaf on to a wire rack to cool. Serve with butter.

Enriched Coffee Bread

● Grease two or three baking (cookie) sheets, according to size. Crumble the yeast in the mixing bowl and cream it with a little of the milk (adding 1 teaspoon sugar if dried yeast is used). Set the dried yeast liquid aside for 10 minutes until frothy. Pour the melted fat and the rest of the milk into the yeast liquid in the mixing bowl. Stir in the salt, sugar, cardamom (if used) and about half the flour. Add the egg and then the remaining flour by degrees. Work the dough until non-sticky, smooth and shiny. Cover the dough in the bowl with oiled polythene (plastic) and allow to prove until doubled in size, about 1¼ hours.

● Work the dough in the bowl, then turn it on to a lightly floured board and knead it until smooth. Divide the dough into three portions. Divide each portion into three equal parts and roll these out until they are about 16 in/40 cm in length. Plait (braid) the strands. Repeat the procedure with the two remaining portions. Put the plaits (braids) on to the baking (cookie) sheets, cover with oiled polythene (plastic) and let them rise for about 45 minutes. Remove the polythene (plastic), brush the plaits (braids) with egg and sprinkle with sugar and almonds. Bake for about 20 minutes. Cool on a wire rack.

Almond Bread Ring

INGREDIENTS

2 tsp/25 g/1 oz fresh yeast or 1 tbsp/15 g/½ oz dried yeast
and ½ tsp sugar

1¼ cups/300 ml/½ pint warm milk (or thin cream)

½ cup/100 g/4 oz butter, melted and cooled

½ tsp salt

2 tbsp sugar

1 tsp ground cardamom (optional)

½ beaten egg

3⅓ cups/400 g/14 oz white flour

5 tbsp/65 g/2½ oz butter or margarine

⅔ cup/75 g/3 oz sugar

1 cup/150 g/5 oz ground almonds (almond meal)

2 egg yolks

3 tbsp chopped, candied orange peel

½ egg for glazing

crushed sugar cube and almonds for decorating

Oven temperature 200°C/400°F/Gas 6

MAKES 1 COFFEE BREAD RING

● Grease a baking (cookie) sheet. Crumble the yeast into a few tablespoons of the warm milk (adding the ½ teaspoon of sugar if dried yeast is used). Stand the dried yeast aside for 10 minutes until frothy.

● Pour the rest of the milk and the melted butter on to the yeast liquid. Stir in the salt, sugar and cardamom (if used), about half the flour and the half egg. Add the rest of the flour by degrees and work the dough until it is non-sticky and smooth. Cover with oiled polythene (plastic) and leave in a warm place until doubled in size, about 1 hour.

● Cream together the fat and sugar and stir in the almonds, egg yolks and candied orange peel. Punch down the dough, then turn it out on to a floured board and knead it for 5 minutes.

● Roll out the dough into an oblong strip 25 × 50 cm/10 × 20 in. Spread the almond filling over it and roll it up lengthwise like a Swiss roll (jelly roll). Place the roll in a ring shape on the baking sheet with the smooth side uppermost, moistening the two ends of the length with milk to seal the circle. Lightly clip the dough with scissors or slice with a knife at 1 in/2.5 cm. intervals. Cover with oiled polythene (plastic) and allow to prove for 45 minutes. Remove the polythene (plastic), brush with egg and sprinkle with sugar and almonds. Bake for about 20 minutes.

Hot Cross Buns

INGREDIENTS

1 tbsp/25 g/1 oz fresh yeast or 1 tbsp/15 g/½ oz dried yeast and 1 tsp sugar
⅝ cup/150 ml/¼ pint warm milk
⅜ cup/75 ml/3 fl oz warm water
4 cups/450 g/1 lb flour
¼ cup/50 g/2 oz soft brown sugar
1 tsp salt
1½ tsp mixed spice
½ tsp ground cinnamon
½ tsp ground nutmeg
¼ cup/50 g/2 oz butter or margarine, melted and cooled
1 egg, beaten
⅔ cup/100 g/4 oz currants
⅓ cup/50 g/2 oz mixed dried citrus peel
shortcrust pastry leftovers for crosses

TO GLAZE

2 tbsp milk ● 2 tbsp water ● 3 tbsp sugar boiled together for glazing

Oven temperature 220°C/425°F/Gas 7

MAKES 12 BUNS

● Grease and flour two baking (cookie) sheets. Stir the yeast, or dried yeast and sugar, into the mixed warm milk and water. Set aside for 10 minutes until frothy if dried yeast is used. Mix in one-quarter of the flour and leave in a warm place for about 20 minutes until the yeast batter is foamy.

● Mix the remaining flour with the sugar and the rest of the ingredients, stir them all into the yeast batter and mix to a soft dough. Turn on to a lightly floured board and knead until smooth. Return the dough to the warm bowl and cover with a sheet of oiled polythene (plastic). Leave in a warm place until doubled in size, about 1½ hours.

● Divide the dough into 12 pieces and shape them into buns. Arrange them, well spaced, on the baking (cookie) sheets. Cover with oiled polythene (plastic) and allow to rise in a warm place for about 40 minutes.

● Make crosses on top of each bun from shortcrust pastry or make a simple paste from 2 tablespoonfuls each of flour and water. Alternatively, slash the top with a very sharp knife to make a cross shape. Bake for 15–20 minutes until golden brown. Transfer the buns to a wire rack to cool.

● Combine the glaze ingredients in a saucepan and bring to the boil. Brush the buns twice with the hot glaze, then leave to cool. Serve with butter.

Hungarian Crackling Scones

INGREDIENTS
1 tbsp/15 g/½ oz fresh yeast
¼ cup/50 ml/2 fl oz warm milk
3 cups/350 g/12 oz flour
¾ cup/100 g/4 oz pork crackling, chopped into pieces about 2.5 cm/1 in square
1 tsp salt
½ tsp ground black pepper
½ cup/100 g/4 oz lard, melted
3 tbsp sour cream
2 egg yolks
1 egg yolk mixed with 2 tbsp milk or water for glazing
Oven temperature 200°C/400°F/Gas 6
MAKES ABOUT 2 DOZEN

● Dissolve the yeast in the warm milk. Chop or grind the pork cracklings finely. Mix the flour with the cracklings, salt, pepper, melted lard, sour cream and egg yolks. Stir in the yeast mixture and knead well. Set the dough aside, covered with oiled polythene (plastic), until doubled in size, 30–40 minutes. Roll out the dough on a floured board, fold it like puff pastry, let it rest for 10 minutes, then repeat the rolling, folding and resting twice more. Finally roll out the dough to 2½ cm/1 in thick, score the surface with a knife point to make a trellis pattern and cut into 4 cm/1½ in rounds, using a plain cutter.
● Put the crackling rounds on baking (cookie) sheets and brush the tops with the egg yolk and milk or water mixture. Allow the buns to rest for 10–15 minutes before baking for about 25 minutes, until browned. Serve with apéritifs or soup.

Walnut, Apricot and Orange Bread

INGREDIENTS
2 tsp/15 g/½ oz fresh yeast or 1 tbsp/10 g/¼ oz dried yeast and 1 tsp honey
1¼ cups/300 ml/½ pint warm water
4 cups/450 g/1 lb wholewheat flour
1 tsp salt
¼ cup/50 g/2 oz sugar
¼ cup/50 g/2 oz butter or margarine
½ cup/50 g/2 oz chopped walnuts
1¼ cups/175 g/6 oz dried apricots, soaked and chopped
2 tbsp grated orange rind
Oven temperature 220°C/425°F/Gas 7
MAKES 1 LARGE OR 2 SMALL LOAVES

● Grease one large or two small bread tins (pans). Dissolve the yeast (and sugar) in the warm water leaving the dried yeast to become frothy (10 to 15 minutes). Mix the flour with the sugar and salt and rub in the fat. Stir in the yeast liquid and mix to a dough. Turn on to a floured board and knead until smooth. Return the dough to the bowl, cover it with oiled polythene (plastic) and let it prove for about 1 hour until doubled in size. Knead again, working in the nuts, apricots and orange rind. Shape into a loaf (or 2 loaves) and place them in the prepared tin(s) (pan(s)). Cove the dough and prove once more for 40–50 minutes.
● Bake for about 45–50 minutes, depending on the size of the loaf (loaves).
● Allow to cool on a wire rack.

Muffins

INGREDIENTS

1 tbsp/15 g/½ oz fresh yeast or 1 tbsp/10 g/¼ oz dried yeast and 1 tsp honey
1 cup/225 ml/8 fl oz warm water
4 cups/450 g/1 lb white flour
1 tsp salt
2 tbsp/25 g/1 oz butter, melted
2 small eggs, beaten

**Oven temperature 230°C/450°F/Gas 8
for oven-baked muffins**

MAKES 12 MUFFINS

● Grease two baking (cookie) sheets and dust them well with rolled oats (fine oatmeal) or wheatgerm or with cornmeal or semolina. Or heat a greased and floured griddle (or heavy frying pan) if the muffins are to be cooked over top heat.

● Stir the yeast into the warm milk, adding the honey if dried yeast is used. Set the dried yeast liquid aside for 10 minutes until foamy.

● Mix the flour and salt and add the yeast liquid, melted butter and the eggs. Mix to a soft dough in the bowl then turn it out on to a floured board. Knead the dough until it becomes smooth, non-sticky and elastic. Return the dough to the warm bowl. Cover with oiled polythene (plastic) and prove for about 1¼ hours, until doubled in size. Turn the dough on to a lightly floured surface, knead and then roll the dough to 1 cm/½ in thickness. Cover with oiled polythene (plastic) and rest for 5 minutes. Cut into 7.5 cm/3 in rounds with a plain cutter.

● Put the muffins on the baking (cookie) sheets and dust the tops with semolina. Cover with oiled polythene (plastic) and leave to prove for about 40 minutes. Cook the muffins by baking them in the oven for about 10 minutes, turning the muffins over with a palette knife (spatula) after 5 minutes. Or cook the muffins for 5 minutes on each side on the heated griddle. Stack the muffins on a wire rack.

● To serve the muffins, pull them open all around the edges. Leave the halves joined in the centre. Toast them slowly on both sides. Pull the muffins fully apart and place a slice of chilled butter inside. Put the muffin halves together again and serve them hot.

Pumpernickel

Pumpernickel is an eastern European bread which keeps well. Serve with butter and cheese or cured meats.

INGREDIENTS
1 tbsp/25 g/1 oz fresh yeast or 2 tbsp/15 g/½ oz dried yeast and 1 tsp brown sugar
5 cups/1.2 litres/2 pints warm water
1 tbsp molasses
6 cups/675 g/1½ lb wholewheat flour
1 cup/100 g/¼ lb dark rye flour
⅔ cup/65 g/2½ oz buckwheat flour
⅓ cup/50 g/2 oz cornmeal
2 tsp salt
1 cup/225 g/½ lb cooked, mashed potato
1 tsp caraway seeds
1 cup/100 g/¼ lb wholewheat flour (if needed)
Oven temperature 190°C/375°F/Gas 5
MAKES 2 LARGE LOAVES

● Grease two large bread tins (pans). Stir the yeast into one cup of the warm water, adding the brown sugar in the case of dried yeast. Set the dried yeast liquid aside for 10 minutes until frothy.

● Mix the wholewheat flour, molasses, yeast liquid and the rest of the warm water to make a very wet dough. Beat well, knead in the bowl until it becomes smooth and less sticky. Add the rest of the ingredients and mix well. Turn on to a floured board and knead, working in the last cup of wholewheat flour if required. Knead until the dough is smooth and elastic. Return it to the bowl and cover with a sheet of oiled polythene (plastic). Prove in a warm place until doubled in size, 1¼–1½ hours.

● Knock back the dough, divide it into 2 pieces. Shape into loaves and put the dough into the bread tins (pans). Cover the tins with oiled polythene (plastic) and prove once again until doubled in size, about 1 hour. Bake for about 1 hour, remove the loaves from the tins and bake for a further 10–15 minutes. Cool the bread on a wire rack. Keep the bread for 1 or 2 days before slicing.

Malt Bread

Swiss Buns

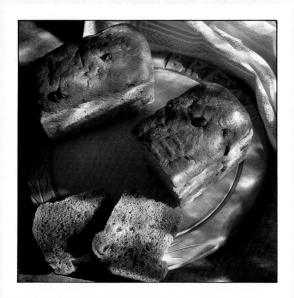

INGREDIENTS
1 tsp/15 g/½ oz fresh yeast or 2 tsp dried yeast and 1 tsp sugar
2½ cups/600 ml/1 pint warm water
4 cups/450 g/1 lb wholewheat flour
1 tsp salt
2 tbsp malt
1 tbsp honey or syrup
2 tbsp vegetable oil
1 cup/150 g/5 oz sultanas (golden raisins)
honey or syrup for glazing
Oven temperature 200°C/400°F/Gas 6 then reduced to 180°C/350°F/Gas 4
MAKES 2 SMALL LOAVES

INGREDIENTS
2 tsp/15 g/½ oz fresh yeast or 1 tbsp/10 g/¼ oz dried yeast and 1 tsp sugar
⅝ cup/150 ml/¼ pint warm milk
2 cups/225 g/½ lb white flour
2 tsp sugar
½ tsp salt
2 tbsp/25 g/1 oz butter or margarine
GLACÉ ICING (FROSTING)
1½ cups/175 g/6 oz icing (confectioner's) sugar
3 tbsp water
colouring (optional)
Oven temperature 220°C/425°F/Gas 7
MAKES 8 BUNS

● Grease two 16 × 9 × 7.5 cm/6½ × 3½ × 3 in bread tins (pans). Mix the yeast (and sugar) in the warm water.

● Add the malt, honey, oil and sultanas (golden raisins) to the warmed flour. Stir in the yeast liquid and mix thoroughly. Put the mixture into the two bread tins (pans).

● Set aside for 1 hour in a warm place, covered with oiled polythene (plastic). Bake at the higher temperature for 15 minutes then reduce to the lower temperature and bake for a further 20 minutes until cooked. A skewer inserted into the centre of the loaf should emerge clean. Place the loaves on a wire rack. Warm a little honey or syrup and brush the tops of the loaves while they are still hot.

● Grease one or two baking (cookie) sheets (according to size). Stir the yeast with the milk, adding 1 teaspoon of sugar in the case of the dried yeast. If the latter, allow the yeast liquid to stand for 10 minutes or so until frothy.

● Mix the flour with the sugar and salt and rub in the fat. Stir in the yeast liquid and mix to a soft dough. Turn on to a lightly floured board and knead thoroughly until the dough loses its stickiness and becomes smooth. Return the dough to the warm bowl, cover with oiled polythene (plastic) and allow to rise until doubled in size, about 1 hour.

● Knock back the dough, divide it into 8 pieces and shape each piece into an oblong 12 cm/5 in long.

● Place the buns on the greased baking (cookie) sheet(s). Cover with oiled polythene (plastic) and allow to prove in a warm place for about 20 minutes. Uncover the buns and bake for about 15 minutes until browned. Lift on to a wire rack to cool. Combine the icing (frosting) ingredients and ice (frost) the buns with it.

Lardy Cake

INGREDIENTS

BASIC DOUGH

1 tbsp/10 g/¼ oz fresh yeast or 1½ tsp dried yeast and
½ tsp sugar

⅝ cup/150 ml/¼ pint warm milk

2 cups/225 g/½ lb white flour

½ tsp salt

2 tbsp/25 g/1 oz lard

FOR THE TOPPING

½ cup/100 g/4 oz lard

½ cup/100 g/4 oz sugar

½ cup/75 g/3 oz sultanas (golden raisins)

1 tsp mixed spice

Oven temperature 220°C/425°F/Gas 7

MAKES 1 LARDY CAKE

● Grease a 20 × 25 cm/8 × 10 in roasting tin (pan). To make the dough, stir the yeast (and sugar if dried yeast is used) into the warm milk. If the yeast is dried let it stand for about 15 minutes until the mixture is frothy. Mix the flour and salt together and rub in the lard. Stir in the yeast liquid to make a soft dough. Turn it on to a floured board and knead until smooth and no longer sticky. Cover the dough with oiled polythene (plastic) and leave to rise until doubled in size, about 1¼ hours. Roll out the dough into a rectangle 1 cm/½ in thick. Divide the lard into three portions and use one-third to dot the top two-thirds of the dough. Mix the topping ingredients together and sprinkle with one-third of the mixture. Fold the bottom, uncovered third of the dough up and the top third down over it. Give the dough a quarter-turn, then repeat the rolling and folding twice more with the remaining topping mixture. Roll out the dough to fit the greased tin (pan). Cover and prove in a warm place until light and airy, about 1 hour. Bake for about 40 minutes, until golden brown.

● Cool in the tin (pan) so that melted fat may be reabsorbed. Turn out on a wire rack. Serve the cake upside-down.

NOTE: Milk bread dough   may be used   instead of the basic bun dough, if preferred.

Cheese Bread

INGREDIENTS

2 tsp/15 g/½ oz fresh yeast or 1 tbsp/10 g/¼ oz dried yeast and ½ tsp sugar

1¼ cups/300 ml/½ pint warm water

4 cups/450 g/1 lb white flour

1 tsp salt

¼ tsp cayenne pepper

½ tsp dry mustard powder or 2 tsp creamed horseradish

2 tbsp chives

1 tbsp/15 g/½ oz butter or margarine

1 cup/100 g/4 oz finely grated (shredded) Cheddar cheese

beaten egg or milk for glazing

1–2 tbsp grated cheese for decorating (optional)

Oven temperature 200°C/400°F/Gas 6

MAKES 1 LARGE OR 2 SMALL LOAVES

● Grease one large or two small bread tins (pans). Stir the yeast into the warm water, adding sugar if dried yeast is used.

● Stand the dried yeast liquid for 10 minutes to become frothy.

● Put the flour, salt, cayenne pepper, mustard and chives into a bowl and rub in the fat. Stir in the cheese and then the yeast liquid (and horseradish if used). Work together to make a dough. Turn the dough on to a floured board and knead until smooth and non-sticky.

● Return to the bowl, cover with oiled polythene (plastic) and leave to prove for 1 hour until doubled in size. Knock back the dough and shape into 1 large or 2 small loaves. Place the shaped dough in the tin(s) (pan(s)). Brush the dough with beaten egg or milk. Cover the tin(s) (pan(s)) with oiled polythene (plastic) and prove in a warm place for about 45 minutes.

● Sprinkle the bread dough with grated cheese if desired.

● Bake for about 40 minutes until brown. Turn out and cool the bread on a wire rack.

● This bread makes delicious toast and may be used as a quick pizza base.

Stollen

● Grease one or two baking (cookie) sheets, depending on size. Crumble the fresh yeast in the mixing bowl and dissolve it in a few tablespoons of the cream. (Dissolve dried yeast with the teaspoon of sugar in the warm water. Set aside for 10 minutes until frothy.)

● Warm the rest of the cream and pour it on to the yeast. Stir in the flour, a little at a time and work the dough until it is smooth. Sprinkle a little flour on top, cover with oiled polythene (plastic) and leave the dough to rise until it has doubled in size, about 1¼ hours.

● Cream the fat and sugar until fluffy and add the salt, lemon peel, cardamom and nutmeg. Work the mixture into the yeast dough and add the dried fruit and almonds. Extra flour may be beaten in if necessary, the dough should be fairly stiff. Allow to rise once again, for 30–40 minutes, covered with oiled polythene (plastic).

● Knead the dough and divide it into 2 or 4 parts. Shape them into round balls, flatten them a little and then fold them in the middle to make half-moons. Place the shaped dough on to the baking (cookie) sheets, cover with oiled polythene (plastic) and leave to rise for about 40 minutes. Bake for 20–30 minutes until browned and cooked when tested with a skewer. Brush the Stollen with melted butter as soon as they are baked.

● Allow them to cool slightly on the baking (cookie) sheet(s). Dip the tops of the Stollen into the icing sugar so that they are completely covered. The bread surface is then sealed by the butter-and-sugar coatings and the Stollen keep well.

INGREDIENTS

2 tbsp/50 g/2 oz fresh yeast or 4 tbsp/25 g/1 oz dried yeast, 1 tsp sugar and 3 tbsp warm water

1⅛ cups/250 ml/9 fl oz single (light) cream

3¼ cups/400 g/14 oz white flour

1¼ cups/300 g/10 oz butter or margarine

⅜ cup/75 g/3 oz sugar

½ tsp salt

1 tsp grated lemon peel

1 tsp ground cardamom

pinch ground nutmeg

1½–2 cups/225–275 g/8–10 oz raisins

¾ cup/100 g/4 oz currants

¾ cup/100 g/4 oz chopped, candied orange peel

¾ cup/100 g/4 oz mixed dried citrus peel, chopped

½ cup/50 g/2 oz almonds, blanched and chopped

melted butter or margarine for glazing

⅔ cup/75 g/3 oz icing (confectioner's) sugar mixed with 1 tbsp vanilla sugar for decoration

Oven temperature 200°C/400°F/Gas 6

MAKES 2 LARGE OR 4 SMALL STOLLEN

Swedish Tea Ring

INGREDIENTS

2 tsp/15 g/½ oz fresh yeast or 1 tbsp/10 g/¼ oz dried yeast and ½ tsp sugar
6 tbsp warm milk
2 cups/225 g/½ lb white flour
½ tsp salt
2 tbsp sugar
2 tbsp/25 g/1 oz butter or margarine
1 egg, beaten
1 tbsp melted butter
4 tbsp coarse sugar crystals or coffee sugar mixed with 2 tsp ground cinnamon or 4 tbsp sweetened apple purée (apple sauce) and 1 tbsp flaked almonds
⅞ cup/100 g/4 oz icing (confectioner's) sugar
2 tbsp water
a few red and green glacé (candied) cherries
Oven temperature 200°C/400°F/Gas 6

MAKES 1 TEA RING

● Grease a baking (cookie) sheet. Stir the yeast (and sugar if dried yeast is used) into the warm milk. Set aside the dried yeast for 10 minutes until frothy. Add one-quarter of the flour to the yeast liquid and leave in a warm place for about 20 minutes.

● Mix the rest of the flour with the salt and sugar and rub in the fat. Add the egg and stir the mixture into the yeast batter to make a soft dough. Turn the dough on to a floured board and knead until smooth, elastic and non-sticky. Return the dough to the warm bowl. Cover with oiled polythene (plastic) and prove for about 1 hour, until doubled in size. Roll out the lightly kneaded dough on a floured board into a rectangular strip 25 × 38 cm/10 × 15 in. Brush the dough with the melted butter and sprinkle the cinnamon sugar over the dough (or spread the apple purée over the dough and sprinkle on the flaked almonds). Roll up the dough like a Swiss roll (jelly roll), starting at the longer side. Transfer the roll to the baking (cookie) sheet and form into a circle. Moisten the ends of the dough with milk and pinch them together. Clip the dough with scissors at 2.5 cm/1 in intervals but without cutting right through. Turn the corners backwards and bend them downwards to make a decorative pattern. Cover the ring with oiled polythene (plastic) and prove for about 45 minutes. Uncover and bake for 20–25 minutes. Transfer the tea ring to a wire rack to cool.

● Mix the icing (confectioner's) sugar and water and ice (frost) the ring. Decorate with cherries.

Swedish Saffron Bread
for Santa Lucia (December 13)

INGREDIENTS

2 tbsp/50 g/2 oz fresh yeast or 4 tbsp/25 g/1 oz dried yeast and 1 tsp sugar

2¼ cups/500 ml/18 fl oz warm milk

1 tsp powdered saffron

about ¾ cup/100–200 g/5–7 oz butter or margarine, melted and cooled

½ tsp salt

⅞–1¼ cups/175–250 g/7–10 oz sugar

1 egg

6½ cups/800 g/1¾ lb white flour

½ cup/50 g/2 oz almonds, blanched and chopped

⅔ cup/75 g/3 oz raisins

½ cup/50 g/2 oz mixed dried citrus peel, chopped

egg for glazing

crushed sugar cubes and chopped almonds or raisins for decorating

Oven temperature 200°C/400°F/Gas 6

MAKES 2 OR 3 SAFFRON LOAVES

● Grease two baking (cookie) sheets. Put the yeast into a mixing bowl with a few tablespoons of the warm milk. If dried yeast is used add the teaspoon of sugar and set aside in a warm place for 10 minutes until frothy.

● Add the fat and the rest of the milk to the yeast liquid. Stir in the saffron, salt, sugar, half the flour, the egg, nuts and dried fruit. Add the rest of the flour by degrees and work the dough until it becomes non-sticky, smooth and shiny. Cover the dough with oiled polythene (plastic) and set aside to prove until doubled in size, about 1 hour. Knead the dough in the bowl then turn it on to a lightly floured board and knead thoroughly until smooth.

● Divide the dough into 2 or 3 rounds and place them on the baking sheets. Cover with oiled polythene (plastic) and allow to rise, about 40 minutes. Brush with egg and sprinkle with sugar and almonds or decorate with raisins.

● Bake for 20–25 minutes. Cool on a wire rack.

Swedish Limpa

Sally Lunn

INGREDIENTS
2 tbsp/50 g/2 oz fresh yeast or 4 tbsp/25g/1 oz dried yeast and 1 tsp sugar
2¼ cups/500 ml/18 fl oz warm milk
4–5 tbsp/50–75 g/2–3 oz butter, melted and cooled
1 tsp salt
3½–7 tbsp/50–100 ml/2½–5 oz treacle/dark corn syrup
5½ cups/725 g/generous 1½ lb rye flour
1¾ cups/scant 250 g/scant ½ lb white flour
2–4 tsp ground aniseed or fennel or 2 tsp ground aniseed, 2 tsp ground fennel, and 1 tsp bitter orange rind, finely chopped
Oven temperature 200°C/400°F/Gas 6 about 30 minutes
MAKES 3 LOAVES

● Grease a large baking (cookie) sheet. Put the yeast into a mixing bowl and cream it with a little of the milk. Add the teaspoon of sugar if dried yeast is used and set it aside for 10 minutes until frothy. Mix the melted fat with the milk, pour it on to the yeast and add the salt, treacle (corn syrup) and spices. Stir in half the rye flour. Add the rest by degrees and the white flour.

● Work the dough until smooth. Cover it with oiled polythene (plastic) and leave to prove until doubled in size, 40–50 minutes. Punch it down then put it on a lightly floured board and knead thoroughly. Divide the dough into 3 and roll into smooth loaves. Put them side by side on the baking sheet with a piece of oiled foil between loaves. Cover the loaves with oiled polythene (plastic) and leave to prove. Prick the loaves with a skewer. Bake for about 30 minutes. Brush them with water twice during and after baking. Wrap the loaves in a clean towel and cool on a rack.

INGREDIENTS
1 tbsp/15 g/½ oz fresh yeast or 2 tsp/10 g/½ oz dried yeast and 1 tsp sugar
1¼ cups/300 ml/½ pint warm milk
4 cups/450 g/1 lb flour
1 tsp salt
2 eggs, beaten
¼ cup/50 g/2 oz butter or margarine, melted and cooled
TO GLAZE
2 tbsp water
2 tbsp sugar
Oven temperature 220°C/425°F/Gas 7
MAKES 2 CAKES

● Grease two 15 cm/6 in cake tins (pans). Stir the fresh yeast (or dried yeast and sugar) into the warm milk. If dried yeast is used, set the bowl aside for 10 minutes until foamy.

● Mix in 1 cup/125 g/4 oz of the flour and leave in a warm place for about 20 minutes until the yeast batter is frothy.

● Mix the remaining flour with the salt and stir into the yeast with the eggs and melted butter. Beat well until a smooth batter is produced. Pour the batter into the cake tins, cover them with oiled polythene (plastic) and leave in a warm place for about 1½ hours until doubled in size.

● Bake for about 20 minutes until nicely browned. Turn the cakes on to a wire rack and brush them with the hot glaze made by boiling the sugar and water together. Allow to cool a little before serving warm with clotted cream or butter.

Swiss Saffron Bread

INGREDIENTS

10 cups/1.2 kg/2½ lb flour

2¼ cups/500 ml/18 fl oz warm milk

3 tbsp/50 g/2 oz yeast or 2 tbsp dried yeast and 1 tsp sugar

½ tsp saffron

2 tsp salt

1 egg

1¼ cups/300 g/10 oz sugar

⅞ cup/200 g/7 oz butter, melted and warm

6 tbsp/30 g/1 oz ground almonds

1 cup/150 g/5 oz raisins

1 egg yolk mixed with 2 tsp water

beaten egg and chopped almonds for decorating

Oven temperature 180°C/350°F/Gas 4

MAKES 2 PLAITS (BRAIDS) OR RINGS

● Grease a large baking (cookie) sheet or two small sheets. Mix the yeast (or dried yeast and sugar) and saffron with the warm milk. Put the flour into a warmed bowl, make a well in the centre and pour in the yeast liquid. Sprinkle a little flour over the liquid and leave to ferment for 10 to 15 minutes in a warm place. Mix together the egg, salt, sugar and melted butter. Add to the dough ingredients and knead thoroughly until smooth. Add the ground almonds and raisins. Cover with oiled polythene (plastic) and leave to rise for about 1 hour until doubled in size. Knock back the dough and leave to prove once again. Divide the dough in half and shape into two plaits (braids) or rings. Place on the sheet(s). Cover and prove once more for 20–30 minutes.

● Brush the breads with beaten egg. Make slashes in the top with a sharp knife and sprinkle the bread with chopped almonds. Bake the breads for about 35 minutes, or until golden-brown.

English Teacakes

INGREDIENTS

1 tbsp/15 g/½ oz fresh yeast or 2 tsp dried yeast and ½ tsp sugar

1¼ cups/300 ml/½ pt warm milk

2 tbsp/25 g/1 oz sugar

4 cups/450 g/1 lb strong white (all-purpose) flour

1 tsp salt

2 tbsp/25 g/1 oz lard

⅓ cup/50 g/2 oz currants

milk for glazing

Oven temperature 220°C/425°F/Gas 7

MAKES 5 TEACAKES

● Grease one large or two small baking (cookie) sheets. Stir the fresh yeast into the warm milk. If dried yeast is used, add it, with ½ teaspoon sugar, to the warm milk and set aside for about 10 minutes until frothy. Mix the sugar, flour and salt and rub in the lard. Add the currants and stir well with the yeast mixture to make a soft dough. Turn on to a lightly floured board and knead thoroughly. Return the dough to the bowl and cover with a lightly oiled sheet of cling film (plastic wrap) or polythene (plastic). Leave to rise for about 1½ hours until double in size.

● Divide the dough into 5 pieces and shape into rounds. Roll out each round to about 13 cm/5 in in diameter and 1 cm/½ in thick. Place well apart on the baking sheet. Cover with cling film (plastic wrap) once again and leave to rise for about 40 minutes.

● Brush the tops with milk and bake for about 20 minutes until nicely browned. Cool on a wire rack. To serve, split the teacakes open, toast them lightly on each side and spread with lots of butter. Eat them hot.